TAKE A WALK ON THE WILD SIDE

TEMBO TAKES CHARGE

BY **THEA FELDMAN**

Design by E. Friedman
Contributing consultant Dr. Robert W. Shumaker
of the Great Ape Trust of Iowa

© 2006 by Meredith Corporation.
First Edition. Printed in the USA.
All rights reserved.
ISBN: 0-696-23289-8
Meredith Books
Des Moines, Iowa

It was another hot day on the African savanna. Tembo looked around. Good, she thought. All her aunties, sisters, cousins, daughters, grandchildren, nieces, and nephews were nearby. The herd was ready for a new day. They were Tembo's herd. Because she was one of the oldest elephants, Tembo was in charge.

That's Elephant-astic!

Elephants live together in close social groups called herds. Usually the elephants in a herd are related to one another. A herd can be as small as three elephants, but most have 20 elephants or more.

Tembo looked off into the distance. She was deciding which way the herd would go to look for food and water. Then she made up her mind and started off. One by one, the rest of the herd followed. Auntie Sala waited for her baby, little Khatiti.

That's Elephant-astic!

An elephant herd is mostly made up of female elephants. Males leave the herd when they mature, around age 11. One of the oldest females is always the head of the herd.

Tembo led her family to a good spot for grazing. There were grasses, bushes, and even trees. Tasty green leaves and stalks were everywhere. Yum! Everyone stopped to eat. And eat.

That's Elephant-astic!

Elephants spend about three-quarters of their day eating. They eat plant parts—everything from leaves and roots to bark and flowers. An adult elephant eats hundreds of pounds of food a day!

Suddenly something startled the herd. Then Auntie Sala saw Boke. The silly little baboon was charging at her again! She knew Boke liked to pretend he was tough—tough enough to even take on an elephant!—but she was not in the mood. Auntie Sala easily shooed the pesky baboon away.

That's Elephant-astic!
Many different animals—including elephants, baboons, zebras, cheetahs, giraffes, and more—live on the African savanna.

Tembo and her sister Jemila were laughing together over Boke's antics when Tembo thought she heard something else. Someone much bigger and much more threatening was heading the herd's way.

That's Elephant·astic!

An elephant's ears are big! An African elephant's ear may weigh 110 pounds and be up to six feet long from top to bottom. When an elephant is frightened, its ears stick out.

Bomani appeared, looming large and close to the herd. The tip of his tail brushed the ground. He flapped his enormous ears and twitched his trunk. Tembo knew it was Bomani from his large size and his deep gray skin. The herd preferred to avoid Bomani because he meant trouble.

That's Elephant-astic!

An adult male African elephant can be 13 feet tall and weigh 15,000 pounds. Adult male elephants live by themselves until it is time to mate.

Tembo gathered her daughters Azize and Fujo and the rest of the family together. The elephants formed a loose circle with the young in the middle. Azize stood over Fujo, and draped her trunk over her. If Bomani wanted a fight, he would have to deal with the whole herd!

That's Elephant-astic!

All the elephants in a herd look out for one another. They help take care of the babies. When danger threatens, the herd gathers together, often forming a circle around the youngest members.

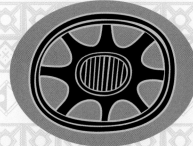

Bomani stood tall. He watched the herd. The herd watched him. No one moved. Then he turned and walked off. Tembo and her family spread out again. Kamou and Kabui, young cousins, trunk wrestled, each dreaming of the day they would be Bomani's size.

That's Elephant·astic!

An elephant's trunk works as a nose—and a hand! An elephant can also drink through its trunk and use it to make noise. Elephants touch each other with trunks, sometimes saying hello and sometimes play fighting.

The sun had climbed higher into the sky. It was so hot! Tembo guided her herd to a mud wallow. A good, relaxing roll in the mud was just what everyone needed.

That's Elephant-astic!
Elephants roll in the mud or toss dust on their backs to protect their skin from the heat and from insects. Elephants are called pachyderms, which is Greek for thick-skinned.

Not far from the mud bath Tembo found a welcome watering hole. The entire herd swallowed trunkful after trunkful of refreshing water. Azize, Auntie Sala, and the others splashed and bathed and dunked themselves in the wonderful water.

That's Elephant-astic!

Elephants use their trunks as straws. An adult elephant can hold two gallons of water in its trunk at one time. Every day, an elephant drinks more than 40 gallons of water.

After they all cooled off at the watering hole, they wandered lazily across the savanna, stopping often to pluck and eat grasses and leaves. Using their tusks, they stripped trees of crunchy, tasty bark. The elephants passed a quiet and calm late afternoon walking and eating. And eating some more.

That's Elephant-astic!

The tusks are really two long teeth! Elephants use their tusks as tools to help them get food and water. They can also use their tusks to fight one another. An elephant's tusks keep growing throughout its life.

As the sun set, Tembo looked around. She could see her entire herd. Good, she thought. We're all here. Ready for a night under the stars after a full—and filling—day!